To Joy Hahn,
All the best,

THE TIME OFFICE

New and Selected Poems

Tom Kelly

Tom Kelly
21/2/12

Red Squirrel Press

First published in the UK in 2012 by
Red Squirrel Press
Holy Jesus Hospital
City Road
Newcastle upon Tyne
United Kingdom
NE1 2AS
www.redsquirrelpress.com

Red Squirrel Press is represented by Inpress Ltd.
www.inpressbooks.co.uk

Cover design by Adam Heslop

A CIP catalogue record is available from the British Library
ISBN: 978-1-906700-35-5

Printed by Martins The Printers
Sea View Works
Spittal
Berwick-upon-Tweed
United Kingdom
TD15 1RS

Acknowledgements

Thanks are due to Andy Croft, Smokestack Books, for publishing
'The Wrong Jarrow' and Sheila Wakefield, Red Squirrel Press,
for the four most recent collections.

Previous collections:

The Wrong Jarrow
Dreamers in a Cold Climate
Love-Lines
Somewhere in Heaven
History Talks

To Sheila Wakefield, Red Squirrel Press, for her continued
encouragement and support.

And to my brother Terry Kelly, once again, for his invaluable
advice on selecting poems for this collection.

Stephen Martin for the Mercantile post card on the cover.

Finally to my family Linda, Bethan, Fiona and Adam with
all my love.

CONTENTS

From *The Wrong Jarrow*

From *Dreamers in a Cold Climate*

From *Love-Lines*

From *Somewhere in Heaven*

From *History Talks*

New Poems

THE WRONG JARROW

The Wrong Jarrow
(Thanks to Andy Willoughby)

In the wrong Jarrow
there's no cobbled streets
no men hunched round corners
eyeing up the ground
there's no gas lamps and hobnailed boots
singing down Ellison Street
there's no one gathering around the Town Hall with banners
and the Bishop Of Durham
isn't saying it's wrong.

It's the wrong Jarrow
the hunger should be more real
like in some African state
trousers should be shiny, threadbare
there should be more hate
policemen should use truncheons more
let's see more blood
broken bones.

This is the wrong Jarrow
poverty needs to be more visible
this is the wrong Jarrow
there's unemployment and deprivation
and no steel works and shipyard and the club's are dead
and there's problem estates and no go areas
and drugs on tap.
But it's the wrong Jarrow
It's not what I want
not what I want at all.
I'll come back when it's burning.

Jarrow Slag Heap, 1933
(From a photograph)

Palmer's shipyard closed.
Three years to the Crusade.
Six years to war.

Working on the Slag Heap,
Palmer's off-white
waste mountain
running through it
dark as blood.

Digging, shovelling.
Hard work.
Low pay.

Poor men working on slag.

The Blood Pit, Jarrow

I've got this photograph blu-tacked on my wall,
five men staring at the camera,
knowing precisely who they are.

It's late in the 1930's; they are at the Blood Pit,
two or three of them are boxers
they've got that look:
hit me, I'll smash you back.

There's one in the middle
that smiles, he must be a manager
of sorts, he has his arms round the others.

No sign of any blood.

My Kind of Town

Bread and lard tastes
so good, fills the belly,
fights cold
that sucks everything,
your desire
to go on, inch on, march on
giving way to anger that pisses like bile, scalds.

There is no way out,
escape impossible,
peel and
strip more pain
-dried skin that's torn into shreds.

At the corner
they kill time
as time kills them.
Nowt.
'Nowt' stamped on foreheads
leaden hands and hearts.

He's working in the timber yard.
Not living at home.
Surviving that's all and bitterness
a ball stuck in his throat
and no matter how much he coughs
it's still there even as I watched his eyes grey,
mist like mercury he could have ladled out.

Did he dream of creeping into their warm homes,
house settling into comfortable sleep
warmth drifting into the loft where a rocking horse eyes him
raise their bedclothes and lift pillows
see them struggle to death. Someone must pay
he snarls at the gaping wound of hunger that eats him
every day and night and he prays dreams
will spread solace through just one day. One day. Please.
Not a lot to ask.

Granny is hit again. Tears prickle
down her cheeks. I feel my legs
and rub away her pain but I can't. Of course I can't.
The stick comes down again.
Men did that then: raise you hand, lift your fist
and bury it in your face. Feel her hurt.

And there's blood on the streets
the polis is dragging Wilfie Page,
the crowd are shouting
and me dad's there.

My town's got blood on the streets,
they're reading the Riot Act
and hunger's a badge posted
on every stomach.

There's blood on the cobbles
as he's dragged by his feet to the cells,
blood on the streets
in my town.

Message on a Bottle

Seaham Colliery explosion 1880

Singing hymns with his son
in that sad enclave,
scratching love-lines on a tin water bottle
'Learn the children to pray for me,'
death inevitable as the failing light
that smudged forty men and boys.

Today I told my daughter
this stone was coal,
gave warmth,
burning like a prayer
in the cold dark.

The River Again

The river's mute, an ex-caulker-burner
knows he's a dinosaur
walking his security guard beat
when a shovel of memories
hits him hard, has him floored
rekindling flames
of his trade he knows is extinct.

A voice on a tape, an out-take from history
struck like a wet clout,
shocking me into the past,
my struggling voice remembered
in the nooks and crannies
that make up your past:
shipyard, river bank, back streets
beat and heart beat of a thousand workers
slamming streets;
women clasp corners
waiting for their men
feeling like catchers
grabbing white hot rivets of money
before their men spend wages on anything
but on what they should.

Waiting
(For Swan Hunters, Hawthorn Leslies, Palmers...)

The bus stop has fewer passengers waiting
at seven o'clock in the morning.

More women now,
they huddle and flick cigarettes
that pin prick the gloom,
odd laughs hitting the silence.

The yards are finished.
Kids need to be told where the river is
and the cranes aren't a fairground.

Some still believe
the river will return:
tankers and refits, the lot!

Delusions,
and fewer passengers are waiting.

Another Time, Another Place

He fancied a walk:
park awash
with drifting kids
and dogs.

He didn't notice:
houses demolished,
the steel works rubble,
river and steel blue sky.

He didn't notice himself:
battered brown mac,
black slip-ons, slipping off his feet,
grey trousers creased
above his ankles.

Under his dead eyes,
soft hands shoved in his pockets,
he had a picture
different from this.

John Donne in Jarrow

Not that long ago,
on my way to the pub,
I saw a man standing at his back door
looking at the sky,
examining early evening light,
flying past
into his dark kitchen.
I imagined thick grease around a cooker,
windows closed tight
but for that moment
he appeared in a great world of air and angels.

Their River

A female Fagin selling drugs,
drinking, flirting and nodding sagely
to boys that could be her sons,
watching their eyes droop,
heavy as broken doors, smashed windows...

One of this merry band
lifts a pint, taking minutes to reach his lips,
then steadily, carefully, returning it
to the beer mat,
he smiles with satisfaction:
a job well done.

The old men watch, they have worked
in factories, on the river, built heavy machines,
broken nails and fingers,
shake their heads at young men sold
up and down their river.

Nostalgia Kid

Twenty years ago it was milk & honey,
Garden of Eden had nothing on those days.
Beer two pence a pint, everybody smiled,
you know I'm right, kids were great. Not like now.
I didn't feel the cold and
I couldn't stop smiling and you know it's true.
You knew me, what I was like, the life and soul
of all-night parties, money not a problem.
Friends would ring day and night: the clubs were jumping.
Best years of me life: nothing like now. Shit days.
Everything's dead, like a bloody cemetery.
You could live, not like now: go on buy me a pint.

Shadows

See them
tripping out the pub
ready for a fight,
belligerence an art form:
the snarl, half-closed eyes,
spitting too near
and then they disappear
pissing off down an alley
lost in shadows
that turn up
in your dreams.

Elegy

The yard's
dead, quiet

chains no longer
hold onto ships
onto lives.

Poems inspired by the paintings and drawings of Spennymoor artist, Norman Cornish

Colliery Road And Man

He's got nowt to tell,
nowt you'd want to hear.

There is light, salvation,
singing in bars and
laughter at home and
all that carry on
but tonight there's drizzle
that dewdrops from his nose
and an ache that burns.

The fence is half-cut,
hitting the field, lying on its back,
it's always like this,

he knows every step
of his road
gets no easier.

Man Alone

I'm drawn to him, something about his nose,
the way he holds his hands, remembering a caress years away.
His eyes are masked but you know they are not with you.

The bar's busy
but he's alone. No smile for the camera,
disappointment anoints him,
might-have-beens tear him to shreds.

He is outside every company, "He's best ignored,"
somebody once said. He wears a muffler
and his shirts worn out. His ex-working hands
soft as a bairns as he searches for a callous
to recall who he was. All he finds is an old man's hands.

Misty Day

Looking up Edward Street
mist holds St Paul's Church,
traps that crown at the top of the street.
A woman pushes a pram and drags an older child
who wants to be anywhere but there.
All the windows are grey, no colour
to redress the scene.

You hear notes of near silence,
the woman's receding stilettos, child's cry,
you feel the church will go, a conjurers sleight of hand,
there would just be a gap, a new vista, the mist extended
with no one answering.

This is the moment before it goes,
the time you will remember before the history bailiffs
do a reconstruction brick-by-brick,
rebuild a world, make memory of this.

Two Women

Two large sherries for the big ladies in their seats.
They know everyone, by their coughs and walks and
everyone knows them. Conversation's a leaky tap, and
a nod, wink, twist of a mouth is all that's needed.

By themselves now, they make do with each other.

A son comes in on a Thursday night, sends over a drink,
they return weak smiles.

Three drinks before the shuffle from behind their table.
They go their separate ways at the corner, the sherry a chalice,
warming them, lulling them into drowsy sleep.

'See ya tomorrow.' 'If ah'm spared,' they don't say.

Telegraph Poles

I'd pray if I wasn't so tired and lie down here and sleep
in these fields if I could. Me hands are tender,
my fingers won't unite in prayer.
I'm not old.
Hunger's clawing at me. The street's moving away
like a dream. Christ's mad on the cross and he hasn't had a shift
and I'm full as hell. That's where I'll end up thinking like that.
Pray for me dear wife. God aa'm clammin'.

Three Men

Three bandy-legged men,
haversacks propped
on aching backs
nod their heads home
close as sin,
telling their tale, reliving the shift
before they go.

They live as close as can be,
fighting elements
living on the brink
that can blast them away,
they know only the moment counts.

DREAMERS IN A COLD CLIMATE

Dreamers In A Cold Climate

speak when spoken to,
worry when teachers shout,
working with slow children they are patient,
sit at the front
away from trouble at the back of the class.

They are the quiet ones
dreamers,
ignoring digs in the back
from classroom terrorists.

They tell the time to slow learners
as time runs away from them.

A Lesson in Killing

The rabbits hung from the backyard line,
fleshy-grey blankets brushed against my head
before I struggled with tears
up the back wooden stairs.

We bred rabbits,
stuck them in wooden hutches,
cleaned out brown marbles of shit:
I didn't know 'bred' meant kill.

Faking It

My world was so small,
cramped in a matchbox,
made of poor egg shells.

Words were underlined,
embossed, still born,
disabled, broken:
aching desire,
rancid, shamed,
life there, faking it.

The Perfect Dream

That incredible tremble of anticipation,
the pain of wanting something
so badly,
tomorrow's infinity,
it must happen now.

Make notes,
plan the future:
"Buy shirt, go to dance."

My list folded,
a neat but perfect dream,
in my inside pocket.

Unmarked

"Me mam says she's not in,"
the debt collector
knowing me mam's stiff and silent
in the back room
looking sternly out at the garden
awake to the collector's reply
he spits out moving back up the path away from us,
his black book unmarked.

The Story Of My Life

You can squeeze the atmosphere,
produce samples that would eat metal.

My dad's eating and making a noise
and I can't cut it out. Today I can't.

I want to scream
out of the street. I sit and
I'm choking. We stare ahead
way beyond language, primeval grunts
blocked in our throats as Alma Cogan sings
'The Story of My Life' and the Bakelite switch
on the Rediffusion points at me.

Geordie

Geordie's been at the works for twenty years,
it's closing, going to China.
He packed the factory away,
wooden crates, machinery coffins.

The young ones started getting other jobs,
he was the skeleton staff.

Production stopped:
silence hummed day and night shifts.
He found a cubby-hole,
got his head down,
nobody bothered him.

The foreman asked him if he fancied China?

He cherished his tools,
measuring everything to a thousandth.

Dreamed about getting it right,
woke sweating,
fell asleep in front of the telly.

Broke his heart seeing tools rattling in skips,
throwing your life away,
eyes glinting with precise memories.

The management said,
'Finish when you like.'
He didn't like,
stayed another month.

He was going to leave Friday,
but lost heart.

The security man
didn't know him
walking out the gate on Tuesday,
severance money and pension
in the post.

The foreman said,
"Aa've known ye years."
Geordie had a better way of saying it,
hate would have featured.

Never said:
"Aa've been a good worker,"
"kept this place going,"
"lost only two days work in years,"
"been here when you were dying."

Just said:
"leave when ya finished."
He left with lead weights
in his head.

He told his wife,
she cried
for what the foreman didn't say.

He wonders where it's gone,
strong beer helps regret.
Not bothered about eating,
long as he gets a few pints
over the dozen.

He finds excuses to go to the bar,
somebody said,
"See aa god about aa man."

"What happened?"

Failing light
on golden moments
he hoped for.

Aa luved sorving me apprenticeship.
In th' yards. Aa fitter.
Hard in th' winter,
freeze ya balls off.

Aa went ti' sea when aa came out me time.
Right roond th' world.

Half th' time aal ya saw wor bars
near th' docks.
60's and 70's:
home wi' enough money ti' choke aa donkey.
Aa was out everee neet.
Then back t' sea.

We wor still building ships,
steelworks, pits, th' lot.
Look at it now.
Makes ye cry.

Bobby Thompson
used ti' make me cry laughin.
He told th' same jokes,
they wor still funny.

Upstairs at th' club,
ya'd see turns off th' telly,
aa saw th' lot.
Aa luved it.

Now? What wi got?
Bloody bingo and karaoke.
Th' Japanese took wa ships,
giv'us bloody karaoke.
Not much of aa swop.

Wi' had jobs.
Ya worked wi' ya fathaa,
uncles, went ti' th' clubs
wi'them,
got aa kick up th' arse
if ya worked yasel.

Aa joined th' club
on me eighteenth birthday.
Clubs are deed,
like th' yards.

We wor proud Geordies.
What wor th' forst words Jimmy Carter spoke
in England?
"Howay th' lads."
May 6th, 1977,
our lass's borthday.

Aa got hor, 'Knowing Me, Knowing You,'
Abba. It was in th' charts.
That was th' last record aa bought.
Same year as th' Queen's Jubilee.
Street parties.
Muhammad Ali came.
Now th' get excited if some daft bugger
from 'Big Brother' walks doon th' street.

Aa torned me back and there's nowt:
small factories and karaoke.
Don't knaa where th' years hav' gone.

Aa used ti' work on th' rigs,
four weeks on and two weeks off: great.
Used ti' call us th', 'Geordie millionaires.'
Should hav' bought wa house then,
spent money like waataa.

Then wa had Thatcher.
Aa hope sh' rots in hell,
deserves to.

Th' see what she's done now
-caused havoc.
Lads divvint work wi th' fathaas.
Things aa was talkin' aboot,
aal gone.
Thatcher was shameless.
Greed: mak' th' rich richor.
"Where'd that leave us?"
Ask every miner,
steel workers at Consett,
shipyards: aal gone.
Black days and neets.

Mind aa loved constant neet shift,
betta money, plenty time t' drink.
Nivvor needed much sleep.

He says he's still on shifts,
clocking-off at closing time.

Bus pass a precious medallion,
saves him money to buy more drink.
That's the bottom line, he doesn't say.

He's got the grey look, seen it in others,
they sit beside him in the bar,
secure together, close as Christmas lights.
Signing on the dole
for the first time in twenty years,
felt awkward.

A week later they said,
"Car park attendant, uniform free.
Eight-till-five.
Monday-to-Friday."
He missed the interview.
He rang an agency.
They wanted his mobile number.
He said, "Aa'll ring ye."

He dragged his overalls out the washing machine,
navy blue intestines struggling
on the line,
they did impossible acrobatics,
wild escaping-from-work-dance.

Held them close,
cuffs worn,
pockets sagging,
arse a fat inverted question mark.

Folded them neatly in a bag,
threw them in the cupboard under the stairs,
the works still on them.

'How aa'm managing?'
Great. Finished months ago.
Sun's shining, what more di ye want?

He misses the routine:
coffee, bus, clock-in early,
two half-shifts, Saturday, Sunday over-time.

He's mowed the garden twice.
Never done that.
Days stretch, they've never done that.

Needs to shave,
remembers more
than he wants.

His wife's
moving away,
he struggles
to get closer.

Writes his betting slips in capitals,
never written a letter in years.

Holds a pencil,
brings it to his lips,
licks the lead,
finds plenty of losers.

He started to think about what he had lost.
Dug into his memories for comfort.

Me fathaa was in th' docking squad,
ma got used t' pushin' him out o' bed
in th' middle of th' neet,
gropin' in th' dark hours,
tumbling doon wooden stairs
hittin' th' cold air
forra annotha docking,
street gas lights
blue an' gold
on th' hunched men
and me da.

Mam'd fumble in da's pockets,
silvor to th' light,
shoved coins in hor purse,
back t' sleep,
richer
for th' dockin.'

Aa don't knaa
if aa'm remembering
or if aa've bin told
and it's aa tale,
not memory,
aa divvent knaa.

No one's ever said,
"You're his double,"
"He couldn't deny you."
Held-in-smile, black hair,
stranger in a photograph,
all he's ever been.

He'd like to talk to him,
have a pint,
introduce him,
"me fathaa."

The father he never had
silent in his wallet.

His son looks like his mam,
sees him now and again.

Got his own life,
never wants to stay
in his company.

He calls
with his kids, they speak French, German.
They never talk.

Half-ten's hard,
bars haven't properly opened, nobody
he wants to drink with.

At eleven, sitting in his usual seat,
sun's a sabre, cutting through the bar's frosted glass;
funnel of light above the snooker table
sees him squinting down his fourth pint at twelve.

A newspaper struggles in his jacket pocket,
winners squared in thick pencil.

"Aa'll gan home early," he tries to say.
A quiet rush of amateur dinner-time drinkers,
next thing it's three,
he's smiling at the barmaid,
drinking as if it's going out of fashion.

Smoking at the bar door,
church clock hits six,
he heads back, a procession of one.

Stood there. Proud as Punch.
Grandfather again.
Brought a sealed envelope
with one hundred pounds
and a plastic bag sweating with cans of lager.

He held the baby, everything fixed,
resolved, complete.

Great night. Could have been longer,
drink got the better of him,
hand welded to a can
in the early taxi.

He has a cup of tea at four in the morning,
curtains open,
near-empty street reflecting him.

Looking at each house
as if for the first time,
wondering what people do,
how they manage.

His shadow escapes on the new carpet,
runs out beside the unlit fire.

The redundancy holiday dream
was a nightmare:
guided tours with a Methodist couple,
wife loved them and
his back was 'giving it six nowt.'
Forty odd years of praying to machines,
crawling under crankshafts,
he's got 'aa back you'd kill for.'

Climbing cathedral steps,
castle walls,
throat dry as sticks,
Methodists' kept smiling.

He dreamed:
euthanasia and lager.

Aa'll hav' t' get aa second black tie,
ah'm wearing this bugger out,
all aa ever do is go to funerals.

Friends from work
share grief and jokes,
badges worn with pride
circling outside the crem.
Twenty minute service,
rest of the day:
drink no tears.

His uncles were Iron Men in the yards,
as a child he imagined nuts and bolts
instead of a head.

Worked the Neptune Yard, Doxfords,
Swan Hunters, Readheads, Hawthorn Leslies,
Pickersgill, Smiths Dock,
all dead now.
He raises a glass, Gobshite says,
"Glad of any excuse forraa drink?"
He's lost for words,
remembering nuts and bolts
instead of a head.

He tried to get to the river,
roads blocked,
barbed, angry factory gates, new estates
ringed with plastic porticoes,
Radio One on tap.

Cranes, legs apart
overseeing, not working,
'oiled for maintenance,'
great Catherine wheels caught in mid-flight,
new estates growing
like fresh plants.
Looking through the ex-yard gate,
mist coughs out the empty dock,
bellies among rubble.

He sees the yard in its heyday,
"Aa Greek boat in forra re-fit."
Prostitutes clatter, white-legged
out the gate, looking everything
out guilty.

Now it's dark.
Yards closed,
River dead,
oily waves panic in a strong tide.

Nobody in the cabins
kicking their heels.

They got their golden handshakes:
new cars, costalot holidays, jobs as security men,
work on the rigs, power stations in Essex. Dole.

A police launch takes over the river
muttering,
seagulls dive
in and out
then away
like the work.
It nags away,
pit of the stomach ache-
has me worried,
he says.

Walls could fall in,
leave only mortar
and me
falling
through air.

Sun smashes windows
on the estate
between bus stop and off-licence.

Shaven heads bow, background figures
shocked in sunlight.

He's seeing something else.
His growing silence stuns.
Light's slipping through curtains,
running down their bedroom wall.

His mother used to make shadow puppets,
rabbits, monsters, the lot!

Scanning his wall
loss
impales.

The broken-up river
gets him thinking.

Sees his mother,
smells her.

The picture isn't breaking-up
not like the telly
when he first got married.

It's clear, restored,
trouble is, it doesn't make any sense.

Nae drink today.
Buy aa paper, well, reed one
in th' library: 'Jobs Section.'
Aa've aalways had aa good eye, steady hand,
canny mover, won the 1958 Whitley Bay Twist Championship:
brain surgeon or lap dancer.

"Best Happy Hour?"
Lasted aal day,
landlord, kept shouting,
"One more hour."

When th' bairns wor born.
Day aa got married,
had ti' say that!

Th' last grandbairn's borthday,
wasn't aa fight til after tea.
Police said, 'family dispute.'
Our Peter paid for th' glazing.

What got him thinking
was his wife.
She said, "Going to see your friends in the bar?"
She has a really good friend,
go everywhere together,
like sisters.

He thought
about having a best friend,
not from the bar,
somebody ordinary.
He never invented a friend
as a child,
maybe he's never needed one.

Mornings: cup o' tea
at th' back door,
feel th' cold
pushin' ya arm in ya coat sleeve.

Cigarette smoke wavin'
ti no-one.

Knaa each face on th' bus.

Heart warm
as toast
by me empty cup.

"Th' porfect moment?"
Rubbing me hands together,
Swarfega makin' them soft, oily,
in th' deed hours,
machines grumbling,
prayin' th' not ganna stop.

Aa'd find somewhere,
tak' aa deep breath,
breathe easy,
porfect.

Nivvor took much notice of me neighbours:
barking dogs,
New Year drink,
fights over th' bairns.

Didn't see them,
day or neet shift
for years.

They nod,
aa don't
knaa them.

Aa followed lights
headin' doon th' valley,
year-after-year.
Rain, hail, over-time,
aa was there.
Trouble is
what de ya dee
when you're not?
Unions are aa waste,
Maggie saw ti' that.
Take what ya given.
Like football on th' telly,
watch when th' say.
Aall aboot advertising money.
'Politics?' Ye can't tell th' difference.
'Footbaall!'
Th' ones' wi' money win.
Our lass out.
Day-time telly crucifies
ya heed.

In his pyjamas,
he checks the clock again,
time's a hindrance.

He trawls rooms.
Letters spring through the letterbox,
criss-cross the unwelcome mat.

Radio and TV murmur.
He listens to next door's silence.
A dog barks without breathing.
Rain was the last straw.

Aa bairn ran doon th' street.
Telephone deed.

The girl in the library helped him
get on-line.
Printed the form,
folded neatly
in his inside pocket.

He couldn't stand its neatness.
His wife wrote her shopping list,
didn't turn it over,
see the empty spaces.

Kids play at the corner
in between cars,
their light-as-air ball skims toward him,
he positions himself, strokes the ball with his instep
back to their age,
the ball runs away from him.
He fell asleep on the bus,
somebody was reading,
'The Kandy-Kolored Tangerine-Flake Streamline Baby,'
and 'Trams and Buses of the North-East.'

In the background
a song he couldn't put his finger on,
he raised his hand
as if in class
asked, "where wa goin'?"
He was just aware of his wife
smelling his breath
saying, "I've got to get back to work."

He focussed on a crumpled piece of paper
by the side of a wall,
walking home he was hard pressed not to stop
in the middle of the road,
he felt hot and old and believed levitation was possible,
imagined his mother was alive
shouting at him for shitting his trousers,
days were longer than he never imagined,
sneaking by on its fingertips,
searchlights were strapped to his eyes
but he couldn't see a way ahead.

A stranger told him of a constant dream he was having,
in his mouth a cactus began to stir somewhere near his larynx,
his shirt clung and his feet were floating,
he tried to believe he was his dead father,
thought he could tip-toe on water,
saw divine inspiration in street lights
and the lager can in his pocket began singing,
'Songs From The Shows,'
and they gave him an invitation to a musical,
'The Marriage Feast of Cana,'
and he sensed his blood was being drawn from him,
sinking into concrete slabs
lined up outside the fish and chip shop.
A woman pressed pound coins into his eyes,
kept saying she had lost her purse on the bus.
Everything was racing and still, silent and opaque,
so alive and dead,
that's when he turned
into a pillar of salt
and began to shout, "Not aa lot aa can do."

They rang his wife at work,
she stayed with him
until his eyes opened.

"Doesn't matter what you do, do it well,"
his mother said.

It had stood him in good stead.
Forty-odd years of work,
those words stayed.

Foreman with power fixations,
self-obsessive managers
with degrees in ignorance,
his motto kept him going.
'How de ye do nowt well?'

This is th' picture aa want:
smiling, pint in me hand.
Our lass wi' her aa arm roond me.

Then aa lie in grass, dead warm,
sleeping but know everything round us.

When aa get up: blue sky.
Me mother holds me close.
Ah'm aa bairn.
Just tha' job.

Got th' chance of aa job. Neet shift.
In aa pet shop. Cleaning oot cages, what have ye.
Th' give ya gloves and aa mask. Aye like aa vet.
Th' die in tha cages. Stiff hamsters
and budgies, parrots. Incinerate them. Wouldn't like that.
They haven't had much of a life on them wheels,
cages, day and neet.

"Think of aa porfect moment?"
Reet…got it!
Aa stood at th' top o' th' street, looked at th' river,
distant, lovelee.
Aa knew what th' whole carry-on, life, was aboot.
Flick of aa switch. Click of aa finger, gone.

Have ye ever read aa book that said,
"This what ye should de?"
Aye "self-help."
Aa looked for one for years.

"Philosophy, a solution?"
Araldite's th' only solution aa knaa.
Aa'v bin heor before:
up an alley,
cul-de-sac,
neor
not quite there.

Aa love me wife
more than she loves me.
Nivvor said that aafore.

That's aa good enough reason
for being heor
on th' edge.

"Luv?" Aa luv bein in th' bar. Pool table, telly too loud,
walkin' in, ordering aa pint. Smoking at th' door,
wind blowing round me arse. Havin' aa bloody good laugh.

"Need t' work?" Aye.
"Pavlov's dog?" Did it win at Crufts?
Ah'm joking. Aaa knaa what yaa saying.
"Life after work?" What sort of life?

New work boots aalways hort.
Leather awkward, stiff,
th' divven't give.
They're lying in th' shed,
gathering dust.
Noticed th' other day,
remembered th' hort,
it's aa pain lookin' at them.

"Need to find something?"
One lad gotta motor bike,
went ti' France, their lass on th' back.
Had t' weld her off!
Barry plays keyboards.
Matty trumphet.
Ah'm tone deaf. Aa don't drive.
Aal aa've done is work.

He wrote a letter,
placed it in his inside pocket
with the window cleaner's money.
First letter in years.

Shave and bath,
wearing his funeral suit, shoes polished.
Walls started coming in
months ago.
'More ti' life than this,"
he never said.

Billy-no-mates and me
stood in the bar,
with the full-time liar,
said he'd cut Geordie's hedge last week.

We watched TV and played snooker,
multi-skilling as usual.

He didn't show,
whip off a Lone Ranger mask,
shout, "Where's Tonto?"

Geordie stood by the river.
Blackness inviting.

He was measuring everything, like using calliper's
in the Fitting Shop.

Get things straight in me heed,
he said over and over.

He stood so still.

He took the world's longest drag on his cigarette,
coming close to something.

He decided to head back home,
then changed his mind.
He had the window cleaner's money
dancing in his pocket,
seemed a pity to waste it.

LOVE-LINES

The Letter He Didn't Write
(From Tommy Kelly in a German Prisoner Of War
Camp, to his sons, daughter and grandchildren)

I've told you some stories, that's what they're not.
Picture what I say, hold the cold,
put your hand in ice,
fridge will do.

What's worse is not knowing.
It's like that all the time.

Have you got your hand in the fridge?

I prayed for an end. Stop.
My life on pause.

They're all here: French, English, Taffs, Scots,
Geordies like me. Nobody understands us.

I saw the French eat a crow. God, did it squawk.
Never seen anything like that.

Did I tell you about that French officer?
I found him. Hung himself.
In the toilets. Nowt to live for.
That's how it gets you. Scrapes away hope,
stomach knotted.

How's your hand in that fridge?
You've got another five years.

'Carry On' In A Prisoner of War Camp

I am annoyed. I want to ask so much,
why you wearing your uniform
in the prisoner of war camp?
How did the uniform survive? Did you not grow?
Captured at nineteen, two more years
to grow in and out the bloody thing.
You are at the end of the line,
a daft grin. Grinning
in a Stalag bloody camp. Come on.
This is getting more like,
'Carry On' in a prisoner of war camp.
Is that Sid James in the front row?
Give me a break. I'll re-read your story,
a Frenchman hung himself, you found him,
other prisoners ate crow.
Not this bloody laughing.

Kiss

Tonight I kissed my dead father
in my sleep;
he was a reclining Christ,
eyes closed,
skin young, pewter-like.

Tonight I kissed my dead father
in my sleep,
he had turned to stone,
surprised by his metamorphosis,
flying above the flat roofs of Lukes Lane Estate,
long-gone Monkton Cokeworks,
headed for immortality
somewhere near the Elmfield Club.

Tonight I kissed my dead father
in my sleep;
silent as stone he had become,
needing a shave,
adhesive for his false teeth.

Tonight I kissed my dead father
in my sleep;
I tried not to remember but he followed me
pointing his long bony finger,
as I threw back the duvet,
remembered that kiss
I had never given him in life.

Bare Wires

A drum thunders in her stomach.
Getting by is a struggle.
She wants the telephone to ring when she's not crying.
She needs everything to be better.
She sees hope in nothing.

She can't touch anything
without being sick.

She feels the bare wires
in her thin wet hands.

Rare

Half-ten in the morning,
she's watching staff,
hoping for movement:
washing dishes, changing beds,
helping by being there.

We say we're clearing her house,
mention the death of her cousin and
she responds, dullness evaporating,
recalling his Jimmy Cagney ways,
we laugh together: a rare change.

Dog Biscuits

She's got her Larry the Lamb voice on
or Beckett pauses
depending on the day
or night you ring her.

The doctor's weary
of being called out,
she goes to the surgery,
gets antibiotics.

"Big as dog biscuits,"
she says.

Mam And The Dog

"I bet that dog's sick as a pig,"
mam says,
seeing a dog being taken for a drag,
wanting to be somewhere else,
this constitutional not for it.

Does she see herself in the dog?
Her son and his car, her lead
to nowhere she wants to go.

Her face reveals little
dull mask
fixed on a distant dog.

Come To This

Waving from a window,
handkerchief flagging
us down the path and away,
it's not until later
that it hits me,
her flag of truce
she would have never allowed.
I don't cry,
it's come to this
after all the tears.

Mam and Sharon Olds's 'The Father'

Sharon says, "Do you think you didn't bond?"
Mam answers with a question,
"Was ya dad bad for long?"

Sharon begins to answer but is startled by tears,
mam gives her a mug of warm white wine
she drinks without pulling a face.

This is mam's living room: wobbly coffee table,
boxes of pills, doctors' prescription notes for more
of the same, romantic novel, large print, from the library.

Sharon describes, in detail, her father's death:
the hair up his nose, colour of his stools.
Mam says, "Don't talk to me about shite,
aa could write aa book about it."
Sharon says, "I will."

Grandmother Tells Her Tale

standing by the front door
to anyone that happens to pass.
She wants a life of sorts,
I sit by her side, watch, listen.

Picture the child sitting Buddha-like,
knowing nothing but a cold step.
She searches for something beyond this,
I sense her need.

I wish then and now I could help,
useless, providing only company.
Granda, hunched in front of TV,
shouts, "another loser."

She lost two children in childbirth,
one at fifteen with TB: she was used to losing.

You And The Rent Man

Under the tablecloth a rent book,
pound notes inching out, like stiff tongues,
licking my hungry eight-year-old eyes.

The Rent Man was important,
you put your make-up on for him,
smiled whatever he said.
You could hear the jingle of his money bag
as he John Wayne-d up the street.

Granny

in the shipyard,
heavy metal drill
in her right hand,
its point touching the ground
as it scrapes along
beside her for two or three paces
until she hauls it
like a baby over shoulder.

A lady driller,
she's proud of that,
badge of honour:
not Maggie mother,
wife, daughter, but worker
trailing her drill
across sodden shipyard floors.

She held the image all her life,
different from this,
she'd not say
her hands lost in soapy water.

A Letter From James Robert Henderson
Aboard The Wellesley, on the River Tyne, 14th March, 1907.

Me Mother placed me on this training ship,
she cannit look after me.
Ah'm writing this letter with aa thick black vine,
letters tak' ower th' paper.

Today wi scrubbed th' deck in tha rain,
hands hard with tha' months aa've bin heor.

They tell us ta pray,
aa pray ye'll think of me.

Ya grandfather to-be, James Robert Henderson,
aged eight, this day.

In The Distance

Granda could tie knots,
his fingers amazed
as they blurred and stopped
revealing a sculpture.

That moment was magical,
halted my breath.

He'd smack his pipe
look in the distance,
hand over the beautiful keepsake
without looking.

Wrapped Round Me

The call for you came at one in the morning:
silent taxi, singing roads,
maternity hallways, pilots of light,
signalling your birth.

Sealed in an incubator:
unaware of fear, distant slamming doors,
television chained in the empty waiting room.

I listen for any sound to recall,
in some future.
I wait for whatever night decides to bring,
the umbilical cord of enduring love,
wrapped round me forever.

Velvet Sleep

I want the all day buffet of sleep,
return time and again, without broken dreams.
Then more, a full course meal of eight hours,
uninterrupted snoring.
The duvet tastes so sweet,
good enough to eat,
lie all day.

Don't let me go struggling to your crying cot,
my hand swimming through those wooden bars,
hearing your cry subside as I sleep standing up.

I want to eat, drink, devour sleep,
breakfast, dinner, tea.
I am deprived, crying, whinging in a corner.

I want to throw myself on the floor, curl up,
become a child, yes become you, a baby,
give me your gentle movement, your velvet sleep.

Boxed-Out

This is the moment when the world is boxed out:
front door locked, chain hanging like a droopy eye.
Before ten, asleep in your cot,
checked on you seven times.

You are our perfect answer,
we laugh at nothing,
suck lemons,
lose smiles,
stop our jaws aching.

I Want You To Know

your mother wanted you more than anything,
you were the most important thing in her life.

I know the precise moment we wanted you,
how we imagined you were a boy,
called you 'Ned', then you were born nameless.

I want to tell you she loved you,
with a frightening intensity.

I want you to be with her,
would love her to feel this moment,
walk with you now.

Time In The Yard

Playing in the yard,
studying bricks,
inching baby fingers
against brick and mortar,
cut-down warrior
with milk bottle legs
in the sun.

You throw your hat,
it sails,
caught on a sudden breeze,
and you are here,
six-year-old,
no longer a baby,
reading without your finger,
eating with knife and fork,
including me in your stories,
playing with time in the yard.

Hurt You

Everyday balancing practicalities
spinning plates
above my head,
feeling tension
aware they could fall
smash on the floor
have me scrabbling
among china shavings,
that may pierce your feet
cut into your soft soles
hurt you in any way at all.

I Don't Want You To Go

This leaving I can barely spell or say
packing boxes, filling my car
with you, as tears become razors
and then floor me as I pass your room
and then the gasps of pain, disbelief:
I don't want you to go.

It's worse than I imagined or ever wanted to believe,
as I cry at the drop of anyone's hat,
just ring now and say anything:
I don't want you to go.

I'm so nervous I have to fight
to do anything.
I watch my mobile phone,
it's going to explode
if you don't ring:
I don't want you to go.

I want you here annoying me
and coaxing and laughing and smiling
telling me that time has stopped
and that we can live in the past
when everything was perfect,
I want to live that lie:
I don't want you to go.

You

I see you at the mouth of a tunnel,
standing almost perfectly still, a solitary figure
in a black short skirt, white top,
maybe it's a T-shirt, I don't know.

I could have mistaken all of this for a painting,
something primitive,
suggesting a life force.

You remain stationary
until your skirt flutters and you move
to the entrance and it closes behind you.

The Ring

There's a ring in a box,
I see it on your crumpled finger,
ruby red, bold
and you were dying.

There's a memory in that box
and I recall it
fresh as a paper cut,
smarting at the edges.

There's a message
half-finished on a wall,
making no sense,
words abandoned,
for some reason
we will never know.

There's a tangled up dream,
I can't put your finger on the ring,
it moves away
like you.

Mine

Warmth teases out flames of flowers.
I didn't notice them until a pot of yellowness
hit me full in the eyes.

You would have loved to see them,
wouldn't have been a surprise to you,
life-enhancing,
God would have got a mention.
I'm a different kettle of fish,
caught unaware by their gaudiness.

I think of your imagined reactions,
flowers glisten like miniature suns,
nodding, hovering in broken plant pots,
once ours but now all mine.

I Never Thought

I never thought I'd be visiting like this:
dancing aerosol, water in a bottle.

I never thought I would be at a garage,
buying flowers, carnations you always loved.

I never thought it would be: if I have time,
after work and before another drive home.

I never thought I'd be alone in a car,
a bag of mixed blessings juggling in the boot.

I never thought or believed this would be me,
I imagine that you would feel the same: strange.

I never thought I'd be driving through the gates
and down the shaded path to your graveside.

I never thought there'd be days I'd forget you.
I never thought, I never thought, until now.

Some Scars

never leave,
white line on my toe,
cut on Christmas Day.

Just visible hillock,
on my left hand,
boil when I was eight.

Mark on my forehead,
stone
thrown from a house
being demolished.

You.

Somewhere In Heaven

Epiphany on the Jarrow Road

Snow's cracking bones under my feet;
half-six light forgets to rise.

I start to believe I can walk forever,
lonely stranger in a film, circa 1964.

A man on a bike, head a magnet to his wheel,
sways past, following van divots.

Then I rise above the woodyard,
head to the Slacks, Jobling's Gibbet:
I smell pitch,
cling to Jobling,
cry into his battered body,
tears breaking down our cheeks.

Jarrow

And we can return
walk on ice floes
jump from iceberg to ice-creams
in the back of the pictures
rewind the past-
men marching to London
unemployment in grainy black and white-
as we search for something
that flutters with defiance
as another shop is boarded-up
getting used to the dark.

The Good-Bye
(From a Jarrow Crusade Photograph)

He carries a kitbag over his shoulder,
stretches to kiss his daughter,
one farewell out of many.

The child's coat is crumpled,
she holds her father's waistcoat,
sees his smooth face and the crowd beyond.

Clear

The ship's dead in the dry dock,
heavy, sullen,
given life when it groans
out the Tyne to Las Palmas,
Cyprus, Greek Islands,
shimmering in turquoise.

It kneads dock sides, angry metal,
escaping with shipwrights' sweat.

Leaving from a distance
of forty years
the view's true, clear.

Into the Rain

Shipyard's closed,
gates knotted with iron.

Men waited for buses to everywhere:
Newcastle East, West.

Here my father lost three toes,
cut off by metal.

Discoloured nameplates
nodding from half-eaten walls,
we screw our eyes into the rain.

The Truth

The river doesn't seem real:
offshore construction firm,
marina, kids fishing from the Riverside Park,
something's not right,
I can't see it clearly.

I want to shape the scene,
sense of history,
oblique references
to shipbuilding, archaic trades,
use dialect, speak the truth.

Night Shift in The Rain

Car park's dead, bottle banks castle corners,
rain shuffles across empty spaces.

Shopping trolleys block Safeway's exit,
mongrels sniff for action,
high-tail it behind the Co-op.

The security man adores TV,
knowing the hours he'll not live.

Then they arrive, wearing rainbows,
accusing grey,
from a world where melancholia is banned,
minor keys forcibly discouraged,
laughter, optimism obligatory.

Dog can't believe its luck-
reversed and made a God!

They begin to dance, bang drums,
outrageous coloured costumes,
flattering air,
play violins, guitars, such joyful music-
shopping trolleys clapping
a synchronised beat.

This transcendental moment evaporates,
the dog witnessed events,
his tail's unreliable.

The security man lost in a DVD,
the rest, us, too busy
watching rain attacking empty spaces.

Work

gave his life order:
the steelworks, clocking in,
drinking with lads
before and after shifts.

Now work's gone,
two iron billets rust in grass,
forgotten lovers,
the bus trip left years ago.

Dole Figure

He can't find a way
into anything
that matters.

When you've got your back
against a wall
that's falling
you can build nowt.

His head's battered
with nothing
he'd care to talk about.

That Time of Life

His head's in a bacon slicer,
days fraught,
relaxation's off the menu.

He calms himself
rarely.

In his head
great stones.

It will work out
he smiles
holding a gun to his temple.

Everyday

he buys scratch cards,
scraping silver
where fortune lies.

His slippers shuffle,
take on a life of their own.

I see him from a distance
further away
than he ever wanted to be.

Fingertips

There's a balloon blowing up
in his head,
fingers are shovels,
in polite company he knocks over words.

Feet clamped in steel boots,
walking's difficult.

His suit's not made to treasure
it's off the peg left-over.

He thinks before he speaks,
botched-up Esperanto
burbles out.

Writing takes ages,
it's all anagrams.

He believes no-one
now they speak in dreams
that have the smell of reality
on their fingertips.

No French Film

His wife's carrier bags are scales of justice.
It's Wednesday morning and she moves to him.

There's no-one painting the scene,
climbing ivy, window boxes screaming colour,
graffiti banished.

He feels, for a moment, he's in a film,
something French he's fallen asleep in front of,
a crowd with cameras
behind him, filming,
his wife's slowly walking toward him,
he feels so tired and sad and knows
her pain, what she's endured because of his silence;
it's as if he's woken in front of the television,
he struggles to put it off,
extinguish this other life
go to bed
but what he sees is his wife as she struggles home to him.

Emotion

He empties his plastic bag,
places lager cans in the noisy fridge,
wanting them chilled,
drunk before he can think.

A boy kicks a ball
against his door
constantly.

His radio's welded to a foreign station,
static swirling round bare rooms.

Tomorrow will be no different.

Nothing joyous:
no *'In Excelsis Deo.'*

Monotony of days
makes him dribble with emotion.

What he has

wouldn't fit in a thimble,
couldn't excite anyone.
What he carries is money,
there's not much of that.
He's got no credit cards,
no letters of invitation,
doors remain shut.
He's got no answers,
nothing in his pocket,
questions he forgets
knowing too well the answers.
What he hopes for,
there's nothing of that left,
in between the lack of everything
that's what he has.

At Her Feet

He said, 'cut your hair.'
At first she ignored him,
flicking her hair like a wave
behind her. She knew it was turning grey,
split ends sprung like fishing hooks,
lacked lustre.
But cut it?
She began to look closely at herself,
examining her hair, crows' feet round her eyes,
wrinkles, hands and even her feet.

One day she took a pair of scissors,
cut that long hair he always loved
until they could see her skull beneath the near-shaven head
and he cried,
and she held him close
with her beautiful short hair and independence
as full as the bag of hair at her feet.

Thick Rope

His son hung himself.
Burn marks on his neck,
never there for him
too interested in drink
bar of the club
his prison,
can't escape
and his son
hung himself at home,
they said drugs,
his other son's a thief
no time for them,
never mentioned anything
as he drinks with the man with
broken teeth
and permanent cigarette
in his burnt fingers.
I can't stop seeing the son
I never knew
turning on the thick rope.

Sunday in Winter

Rain drills his face,
beer's worn off.

Juke-box yawns light in the empty bar,
this is the worst of times:
afternoon stupors, dank bedrooms.

He watches from the upstairs window,
one slipper shoved on, the other in his hand, like a cosh,
he berates the wall,
head staggering with the shock
of the mess he's living in.

Things were better: children looked up to him,
his wife waited for his return.
Was that him or some stranger's life rifled,
allowed a dream to sneak in,
filch its corrupt way into this unbearable aching.

In the dark hours

wind hollows skin
tight as a drum,
this is the time
when we hold on.

In the dark hours
watch figures climb,
fill fingernails,
scratch against doors
closed long ago.

HISTORY TALKS

History Talks

(Charlie's Park, Jarrow)

In the park renegades dig in the bushes,
fire at missing soldiers as ghosts hit mist.

Struggling round the bandstand
long-dead lovers,
tired of waiting for soldier boys,
killed at Dunkirk or Flanders
without a song hitting their dry lips;
survivors tell tales
in care homes for the profoundly deaf.

The park and lovers faraway,
that day no longer.

I still hear them shushing in the grass,
growing into a shout until pain numbs,
the picture settles
into a ball:
history that will never roll away.

Cold Morning

Crossing fields,
snow firm beneath my shoes,
work round the corner
this cold morning.

Shipyard's deathly quiet:
Time-office fire buckles up the chimney.
Gateman reads Thomas Hood.
Timekeeper sings light opera.

I can't see the future,
imagine anything
apart from this.

Angel

in the shopping centre,
no longer bronzed, walking tall.

You went 'deep sea,'
came back with money, tan.

The bums checked
The Shipping Forecast,
knew where you drank
them stupid.

Now white-haired,
suit needs cleaning,
cashing your giro.

No angel
in the bar
you filled with drink.

Jobling

(Jarrow pitman William Jobling was the last man gibbeted in the north of England in 1832)

Jobling, Jobling,
bell tolls, rolls
to a gibbet
stuck in stone,
inscribes his name:
Jobling, Jobling.

Jarrow Slake:
gulls flag,
Jobling's post
severs sky.
Cranes bow,
lift high
as Jobling's stench
in August sky.

His bowels
left him.
His flesh
left him.
His cage
kept him.

Armstrong hit Fairles,
Jobling was there,
ran to Shields sands,
crowd tried to gaff Jobling
from the uniforms.

Armstrong ran
to sea
breathed his last
on a bed
not a rope.

Jobling's name's plentiful, cheap.
Court laden, verdict known,
judge ladles a rancid law
laced with more.

Judge Parke decides not to dissect
but hang and erect
on Jarrow's Slake,
"We must stop these *illegal proceedings.*"

Jobling's wife, Isabella,
visited Thursday,
carried their child.
He hangs Friday.

A bell rings
welcomes
to the scaffold.
It rains.

Is this death better than sleeping
under stone or flying after gas
in that black hole?

He is roped,
still.
Someone shouts, "Farewell,"
turning extends his suffering,
life, hell.

Dropped, stripped,
smeared in pitch, dumped.
Painted pelt,
week-end worker
fits a metal suit,
breaks Jobling's face,
mask hides any trace
of hammering.

Hepburn, pitmen's leader,
waylaid his men's rage
at Boldon Fell.

Men, women, gaped,
Jobling's procession
pillaged strength.

Stuffed in a barrow,
hauled up the gibbet:
monument to authority.

Isabella,
from her cottage
sees her man:
Jobling, scarecrow,
butting pitmen
back to work.

Jobling's friends
buried him
in his cage.

Union dead,
corpse lies
waiting spring
to rise.

Mary Ann Cotton 1832-1873.

Mary Ann Cotton was hung in Durham Jail in 1873. She allegedly poisoned family, including sixteen of her children.

Mary Ann Cotton Children's Rhyme

"Mary Ann Cotton
She's dead and she's rotten
She lies in her bed
With her eyes wide oppen.
Sing, sing oh what can I sing?
Mary Cotton is tied up with string.
Where. Where? Up in the air
Sellin' black puddens a penny a pair."

Arsenic

Aa blessing in disguise,
pleasure leads ti their pain.

Aa love ti love,
makes life worth living,
time after time:
aa bed's for pleasure.

Wipe tha brow,
feed aa few grammes,
coarsing, jiggling through veins
ti their end.

Arsenic in Broth

Loved aa few men,
gave everything
but there again
that's not aa sin.

Aa woman's place:
stuck in th' home,
but there's disgrace
when ya all alone.

Arsenic in broth
is tha full stop.

Daft Face

Aa knaa me needs:
hide any trace,
give him aa feed,
see his daft face.

Th' big bugga,
aa knaa it's wrong,
there's annottha
comin' along.

Better than nowt,
gives me aa shout.

Me

Feed poison
ti th' bairn,
too many,
less of aa life.

Aa dole out death,
insure th' familee,
money in th' hand;
poison feeds me.

Mary Ann Cotton and the WHY question

Cleaning another shitty-arsed, stuck-up house owner did it?
One piss bowl, outside midden
stinking to high heaven too many, "Yes missus,
aa'll do that. Clean up after ye. Just lie there,
and aa'll do ya biddin."

You had enough shit in your life.
They brought your dead father home in a bag, the colliery name
stamped on the side. You were eight. Your mother made do, mended
married quick to survive, "Ye hav ti have aa man."

One more, "answer the door," being ignored, invisible.
All those 'one mores' mounted. Is that how it was?
You said nothing at your trial, told to be quiet,
ignorance a weapon used against you and your silent kind.

Letter from Mary Ann Cotton, Durham Jail

Aa knaa what ye are up to. Want ti speak to me
before aa swing. Aa knaa ya game.
Aa've read th' papers, seen th' crowds' faces,
"monster," th' shouted. That's stayed wi' me.

Aa've just fed th' bairn, sh' pulled at me breast;
fixed her up with aa good family,
they'll look after her, too late for me:
me neck will stretch, drop like aa broken flower.

De ye want th' truth? How many aa killed?
Put that in ya book, tell th' world.
Aa can see ye. Ye've got me guilty as sin.
What about th' sins played on me?

Ye don't want ti listen. Aa'll say nowt.
Write 'monster'- that'll sell.
Yours, this day, March 24th , 1873,
Mary Ann Cotton.

"Heaven is my Home"
(Mary Ann Cotton's final words)

Strapped, rushed
to the scaffold,
as if wearing callipers,
your legs
attacking ground,
struggling,
a final wild dance
poisoning air.

"The Invisible Ticking of Remorse"

**(From *'By Grand Central Station I Sat Down and Wept'*-
Elizabeth Smart)**

It's what I didn't say and now words hang
like those plastic bags in an Autumn tree,
veils from missing brides; I know it was wrong
for words to be left between you and me,
as year after year I watched time escape,
and now I know, I didn't say enough.
Like Hardy writing thirty years too late,
scribbling in the dark and cutting-up rough.
Tell me can poetry re-make the past?
Does it have that transforming quality?
Do you have a ready answer to that?
And what can and does it achieve for me?
What I didn't say hurts, the knowing shocks,
I can't balance the books; it's loss that costs.

No Laughing Matter

Living next to dread,
close to the lip
of everything but food.

Standing on corners
pushed by police,
poor whites
-violence caged.

1930s hard;
then a wild practical joke,
you're a prisoner of war,
no laughing matter.

You were never surprised
what life threw at you:
quality always poor.

Small Fact

Something about the way
I pushed open the door,
hand at an odd angle,
not noticed that before.

Lingering, unsettling,
an ordinary act
and that is all it seemed,
just a nagging small fact.

It refuses to go,
still here and hanging round:
I'm carrying dad's hand,
lost and now somehow found.

Geordie

First pint went down a treat,
didn't hit the sides,
window cleaner would have to sing
for his coppers.

Things weren't different,
bar looked the same,
manager still never smiled
as he pulled Geordie's sixth pint;
he felt the lining of his inside pocket,
fingers meeting the seam,
nothing left: home on the agenda.

He smirked at the weak afternoon sun,
found a note in his jacket,
folded it into a tight ball,
watched it following the gutter.

His wife was sitting in the back garden,
hair falling on bare shoulders,
heard his key in the door,
saw his fixed smile used for every occasion,
ready-made answer,
"Nevva been betta."

Asleep on top of the bed
when she left for work
without shouting a distant goodbye.

Light burdens the bedroom,
oversees the untidy mess
he's made.
His dreams fresh as cellophane,
innocent, new.

Memories batter him:
pints waited in the bar of 'The Neptune;'
lads running up the bank,
"Plentee work in th' yards."
'Esso Northumbria' sitting on the streets.
All long gone.

Now he's an outsider,
tracks broken up,
stations well gone
like Geordie by half-eight.

He started to drink at home,
more when his wife was at work.
Go to the off-licence,
slippers, the furry ones
that just stayed on his feet.
Can after can chilled his stomach,
heading home
diligent as any priest
before Mass,
focussed on one thing: drink.
The same trip
three times a day,
empties half-moon his chair,
telly loud
as a bad karaoke,
he slips into a stupor,
welcome home present
for his wife
she could do without.

She got him a dog,
cocker spaniel with a limp
from a lass at work.
Thought it would give him something.

In the bar
stunned by lack of desire,
life on a distant horizon.
Suit shiny,
face florid, shoes thin,
belly bulges over his brown belt.

He can't stand
after a bloody good session,
smiling onto the last bus,
eyes swimming.

I missed seeing him,
catching every word in ten,
standing at the door of the club,
eyes screwed at the cars heading home and
night trains spreading light like a Benediction
on the fields and Geordie.

His sons placed him in the past,
grandbairns laughed at his funny walk.

Night was clinging to his day-dreams:
somebody gave him fifty quid,
said drink yourself stupid.
He got three jackets dry cleaned,
(special offer: 3 for 1);
barmaid cut his hair,
barbers was shut,
it was Sunday.
Grey and white hair
lapped his seat.
Wife emptied her purse
into his jacket pocket.
Sons carried him on their shoulders,
he cried with joy.

Day-dreams bruised against the bar,
left him clueless,
legless again. This time
he knew it was a dream.

I met him on the bus,
 "Aa need aa routine,"
I nodded.
He grabbed my arm, spat out,
"Don't take the piss."
Fell asleep. Missed his stop.

Somebody in the club said,
"Security man-constant nights,"
the telephone number
embossed on the stripped beer mat.
His hands rang with sweat.
They said, "Can you start tonight?"
Nothing about wages, hours, even he knew
he was half-cut.
The job was at his old works!
"Full circle," he said in the damp Portakabin,
watching night fall away like a slow pint.

They gave him a yellow jacket, plastic name badge
stuck on his hat.
Punched a card in a machine,
proved he was there at half- two in the morning.

He thought it would happen.
It did, "felt it in me waatta."
They appeared:
factory back in full production,
working over-time, sweating like a bull,
machines back from China,
pallet after pallet
filling the aisles, couldn't get moved,
place swam with light,
metal on metal.

At six the lad from Krakow
shook him awake and made himself a cup of tea
from Geordie's cup.

He only lasted a week,
supervisor smelt his breath
marched him out the gates.
"The last straw?" There's been too many.

He could list things not started.

Knows about depression, "It's when ye've got nowt ye want."

Walks round and ploughs the living room:
Escher in a hamster cage;
submarine in air.

His breath flutters, bald head sweats.
Sees himself, twenty years ago,
on a train, Newcastle to King's Cross,
bag of dirty washing,
cans evaporate.

Done this a thousand times:
'B & B,' 'Full English breakfast.'
Bairns forget him,
fugitive following work.

And then it started on the train:
everybody was somebody he knew!
Work mates, dead uncles, grandfathers.
He saw his uncle Johnny on the Crusade,
icons ploughing through rain.
No one moves, no bores or drunken squaddies.
Wetherby rain etches, self-harming his face,
cries as he weaves his name,
the lip of his can in the space below the lights,
a kind of immortality:
working man on a journey
believing in a dream: better life, a few pints.

They all told their tales:
Great grandfather worked Hebburn and Harton Colliery
from thirteen. He showed his hands,
hard as bell metal, squeezed Geordie's shoulder.
"Th' seams wor only three foot high,
just as well ahm aa small bugger."
He saw his grandfather,
told him about the Wellesley training ship,
stories he wanted to know. How hard it was,
battered by big lads.

Pulled out a photograph of him and his mother,
it was his turn to weep.

"Too much, it's aal too much," he said.
The photograph shaking in Geordie's hand,
was a betting slip rolled into a ball.

His wife called home at dinner-time,
found him asleep in lager cans,
she wanted to do something,
another life,
not just passing time-
she scooped up the cans, put off the gas fire,
closed the door
as their lives fell apart.

When he woke, the street was empty,
she was further away than he knew.

He found cash at the back of a drawer,
photograph of his dad
working in America,
proud and wide as he was tall.
He carried the photo above his head,
as if he had won the Cup,
achieved something,
that's when he cried
great gulps of tears.

Looking for anything
he scattered the last of his lager
on grass outside the club
before it opened.

He wanted change. Something stirring.
He passed the railway crossing, scrap yard,
rippling grey river,
shouted. "That's me last drink,"
a back-up can freezing in his overcoat.

Lager sprayed sighs,
belched sobs of regret,
he suckled the dregs,
anointing his fingers
and made a sign of the cross,
"In nomine Patris, et Filii et Spritus Sancti, Amen."

Stood still:
an altar boy
in the presbytery
before Mass,
the moment he wanted
more than anything:
the edge of memorable.

He had found something
and walked slowly
into the river.

Two days later
a police launch
dragged him out
at the mouth of the Tyne
he could never leave.

New Poems

The Time Office, 1965

In the dock a boat straddles, a big man wearing a too small jacket;
my corduroy trousers run to Chelsea boots,
glowing with impossible dreams as the Tyne ruffles,
nudges nervously dock gates, a pulsing lung,
yet I can barely breathe with ignorance.

The tank cleaners' cigarette smoke crawls from clawed fingers,
they throw cruel jokes, cigarette butts and disappear into toxic;
wrapped in oil, painting everything.
It is all about money: the quicker they work,
the sooner they leave phlegm, rags and buckets of oil.
I calculate their wages, dry figures under ochre light.

At half-two in the morning, shipwrights, labourers, riggers,
embrace a boat, leaving after a refit,
heading out the Tyne without a backward glance to *Amsterdam,
Limassol,* badges rusted to their sterns:
a bad bruise after a rough night.

Workers' bikes creak in hold-your-breath early mornings,
night giving in inch-by-inch to light:
I still see them heading home,
as I whisper lives into a black ledger.

Last Day

The manager past the canteen window,
cigarette packet stuck in his breast pocket, always a bad sign.
"Sorry to keep you." Even worse when he was pleasant.
"Falling sales, world markets,
Thank you for your time. I am sorry."

Five hundred and fifty worked there.
Now down to fifty. I don't know how long they will last.
Had a few drinks,
worked until finishing time.

Wondered

He shook hands with everybody,
kissed the office girl blushing to the roots
of her peroxide hair. Had a fixed smile,
waved too readily for comfort.
"I've always worked," he said. "I know," I didn't say.

Platitudes came easily.
We got back to tidying desks,
looking earnestly at the clock, checking watches:
I wondered what he would do.

Quiet

In the cabin, under the table, a crouching yellow waterproof suit,
drying in patches, underside glistens,
black mud from under a stone.

A security guard sits with his feet up,
hat cavalier fashion,
flask on the empty Formica table.

Wind blows carefully over the Tyne,
yard gate says, *deliveries discontinued*,
padlock, a brown bracelet, security man shouts,
"quiet as the grave."

Family Ties

Make-up's not right,
needs applied evenly.

Eyes move quickly,
startled by how alike we are.

Age spreads features,
resemblance grows.

Your death false,
years fall away.

Call In

My mother would call me in,
day slid into night,
shadows knifed my imagination.

Tonight kids kick each other behind shops,
batter club windows,
run away from no-one at eleven o'clock.

I can't hear my mother's voice
or anyone shouting anything but obscenities.

An Imaginary Family Photograph

Smile at the lens,
if the camera never lies
-will we be exposed?

Imagine it processed:
drowning images,
figures yawning in fairground mirrors
until they are family,
placed in a frame,
brown, gold-leaf trim.

Tell careful stories:
sun made us squint,
light creates shadows,
photographs lie,
nothing like the real thing.

Stranger

He died before I knew him,
like an ancient newspaper
you find under a carpet,
wrinkled out-of-date ticket
in a coat you rarely wear,
somehow you but so distant.
These other peoples' stories
created him: tall, white-haired,
gentle as a kind stranger.

Next

The beach in summer:
cutting wind and sand sting
eyes and bare legs.

On the outside of the circle
Dad sees a pint,
mam's somewhere else,
gaudy, expensive.

We play with uneasy silence,
a 'Picture Post' photograph,
wondering where to go,
what to do next.

The Crying Game

I thought of you today:
cheap make-up,
rouge billowing,
halo on your cheeks.

I thought of you today:
stuck in traffic,
cut off the radio
contending
with silence.

I thought of you today:
decades
after your death,
another world.

I thought of you today:
didn't cry,
tell anyone,
you were with me
all day.

Wicked Man

I'll swing for him, so help me God, I will,
she would tell me as we hunched by the coal fire.
Granda could have been struck down dead
as he put on his bet, smoked his pipe with a smack,
went for two pints on Sunday night.

He's a wicked man.
I never nodded, smiled agreement,
pictured him wicked
until she showed me her ankles.

Mass

I feel God's grace,
see Christ die on the cross.

God's in a box. Trapped,
white monkey in a gold cage.

Praying so hard,
I believe I can levitate,
climb above the altar,
cling to the transfixed statues,
kiss Christ's bleeding feet.

The Holy Ghost

I didn't know;
Christ had thorns stuck in his head,
God Almighty was in everything,
even Goblin pies I hated.

The Holy Ghost a mystery
until he came:
burning coals,
shuggy-boating above my bed,
placing his blood into me.

Smile
(For Father Conlin)

Our priest was a saint,
who else would wear suede boots
turned-up at the toes?

You could taste his prayers;
he bowed to the cross
in the presbytery
with no-one there.

His beatific smile,
like Jimmy Stewart
at the end of, 'It's A Wonderful Life.'

Mass Book

Black leather cover,
indented gold letters,
feeling the Mass Book
dimpling my fingers
meant luxury:
buying with cash,
new suit from Burtons
without weak payments,
silver service upstairs at the Co-op.
I rubbed the book thin as a ghost
that hung round with poverty.

Until the Deaths

Communion a worry,
I side-stepped in my pew,
allowing others to go.

My tar black soul
turning darker,
Confession out the question.

Weeks crept into months of sin.
Bless me Father for I have sinned,
did not feature until the deaths started.

My First Holy Communion Photograph

tells the tale, on the top tier
at the end, standing on a wobbly bench, uncertain,
waiting for Christ to strike me down
if I moved an inch toward sin.

The red sash was blood,
brilliantly placed across my chest
for all to see and know.

I was one of God's children,
chosen to end-up martyred
as Canon Blenkin told the photographer,
Tell them to smile; they're not going to be murdered.
I knew different.

Confession

Bless me Father for I have sinned,
I waited for sin
to pour into my crisp white shirt.

The teacher said,
You've been horrible to your sister,
I repeated the mantra in Confession,
gave my sister pig-tails I pulled.

The shadow priest,
brogue *thick as the bogs,*
granny said,
hoarse-whispered,
Say two, 'Hail Mary's' and one 'Our Father,'
in the years before ten decades of the rosary.

Transubstantiation

Communion wafer
crisp, clagging
my throat.

I could not swallow
walking to the pew,
cutting my knees,
impressed with pain.

The wafer congealed
dried blood.